THE WORLD OF HORSES and PONIES

by Maureen Spurgeon
Illustrated by Robert Morton and George Fryer

KIBWORTH
—BOOKS—

First Published in 1993

Published by Kibworth Books
Imperial Road
Kibworth Beauchamp
Leics LE8 0HR, England

Printed in Belgium

ISBN 0-7239-0071-X

CONTENTS

THE STORY OF THE HORSE

Horses were on Earth long before mankind. When Prehistoric Man began living in caves, the horse as we know it had already been on Earth for at least one million years.

HYRACOTHERIUM

The first horse was about the size of a hare. It fed on shrubs and leaves in the woodlands of Europe, East Asia, and North America 50 million years ago. It is also called Eohippus, or 'Dawn Horse'.

MESOHIPPUS

30 million years ago, Mesohippus, or 'Middle Horse', was as big as one of today's sheep, with longer legs, and three toes on each foot. The middle toe was the beginning of the hoof.

MERYCHIPPUS

Ten million years later, donkey-sized Merychippus, or 'Grazing Horse', was eating grass. Its teeth were longer and better for grinding the tough vegetation.

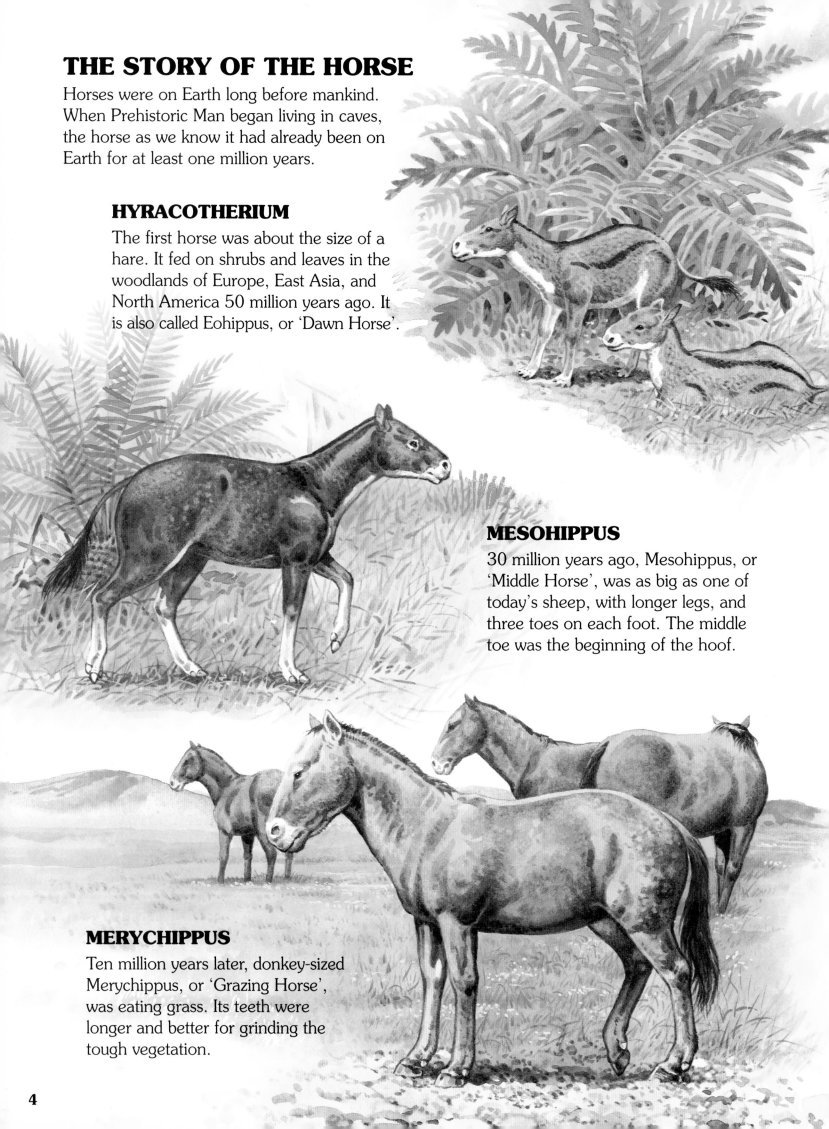

PLIOHIPPUS

Another ten million years later, and the horse was as big as a pony. It had hooves of a kind, and longer legs so that it could flee from danger and travel further for pasture.

EQUUS

With its toe bones fused together into a proper hoof, 'Modern Horse' began living on Earth about two million years ago. It has changed little since then.

5

TYPES OF HORSES

There are many *breeds* of horses, each distinguished by specific colourings and markings, as well as by size, character and body features. In addition, horses and ponies may be classified as various types.

HACK

A hack is a type of horse which is ridden purely for pleasure. Its neck and legs are long and elegant, and its lightweight body makes it the perfect horse for female riders.

EVENTER

An eventer is a horse of many talents! It has to compete in dressage (see pages 26-27), over cross-country courses, and at showjumping – the three sections which make up the competition known as an 'event'.

HUNTER

A hunter can be any horse which is suitable for fox-hunting, hence the name. But a person who is not interested in hunting may choose a hunter for its ability to carry a rider of any weight over any sort of country.

COB

A cob is a type of riding horse, often used for pulling wagons and carriages. Stout and strong, it has a short neck, and short, thick legs.

HORSES AND PONIES ON SHOW

Many horses and ponies love performing for a crowd! As well as for the characteristics of their particular breeds, they are chosen for their stamina, intelligence and obedience.

SHOWJUMPER

Showjumpers are always the lighter breeds of horse, chosen for their quick reactions and ability to work with a rider, as well as for their natural intelligence and talent for jumping.

SHOW PONY

Show ponies are often working ponies, too. 'On show', they may be judged simply as examples of their breed, or ridden over a course in competition with other ponies.

LIBERTY HORSE

This is the name for horses which perform in a circus ring; sometimes working with a 'bareback' rider or riders ('bareback' means riding without a saddle), and sometimes as a troupe of horses without riders.

POLO PONY

These ponies are 'on show' when they are being ridden during the very fast-moving games of polo. As there are fierce collisions between competing ponies during play, they are frequently injured, and polo players must have a 'string' of trained mounts available at all times. A polo pony needs to be supple enough to twist and turn quickly on the field, as well as strong enough to carry a rider.

BASIC TYPES . . . AND WILD HORSES

Today's horses have all developed from three basic, prehistoric types: the Steppe type (see Przewalski's Horse below); the Forest type, which is now extinct; and the Plateau type (see Tarpan below). Most of our finer-boned horses and ponies evolved from the Plateau type. Przewalski's Horse still lives and roams freely in the wild...just! The other 'wild' horses shown here are descended from horses that escaped from man in the past and became wild, or 'feralised'.

TARPAN

The Tarpan died out in the wild in Russia only 100 years ago. A few are still bred nowadays in captivity. The Tarpan is a descendant of the Plateau type of horse.

PRZEWALSKI'S HORSE

(Prish-voll-ski's)

Also called the Mongolian Wild Horse, or Asian Wild Horse, this was named after Colonel Nicolai Przewalski, who, in 1881, discovered a herd, unchanged since the Ice Age. A few, perhaps only 50 or so, still run wild in southwest Mongolia. This horse is a descendant of the prehistoric Steppe type.

BRUMBY

During the Australian Gold Rush in the 1850s, many farmers left home in search of their fortunes. The horses they abandoned became the first Brumbies, the wild horses of Australia. These were joined later by horses turned loose by the farmers who began using machinery, instead of horse power, after the First World War.

MUSTANG

When Hernando Cortez came from Spain to conquer Mexico in 1519, he brought horses with him. From these are descended the Mustangs of the American plains. Mustangs were often rounded up by cowboys for use as cow ponies. An untamed mustang was called a 'bronco'.

CLASSIC HORSES

Classic horses are those breeds which have influenced the breeding of horses throughout the world. Breeders and owners alike see in them the supreme standard of excellence by which to judge their own stocks.

ANDALUSIAN

The Andalusian horse comes from Spain. These great, white horses nearly died out after Napoleon's invasion of Spain in the early years of the last century. The breed was only preserved thanks to some Carthusian monks and a family called Zapata, who concealed a few pure-bred Andalusians from the French invaders.

BARB

The Barb is second only to the Arab as the oldest breed of horse. Pure-bred Barbs are very rare today, and are traditionally ridden by the Berber tribesmen of North Africa.

ARAB

The magnificent Arab horse can be traced back to around 3000BC in the deserts of the Yemen in Arabia. It is the oldest known, pure breed, and most modern breeds owe much of their development to Arab ancestors.

THOROUGHBRED

Although the Thoroughbred is descended from the Arab horse, it has long been regarded as a classic breed in its own right. Racehorses all over the world are from English Thoroughbred stock.

HORSES AROUND THE WORLD

There are many countries in the world which have at least one 'native' breed; that is to say, a breed that comes from just one particular place or area. Four such breeds are shown here.

APPALOOSA

This horse is easily recognised by the raised spots on its coat, especially on the hindquarters. Appaloosa is a corruption of ' Palouse', the name of a river in the American states of Washington, Idaho, and Oregon. The Nez Percé Indians of the region first developed the breed.

CAMARGUE

One of the most famous of all native breeds, the pale grey Camargue horses live in the swampy marshlands of the Rhône delta in southeast France. Now a recognised breed, its origins are shrouded in mystery.

HANOVERIAN

The Hanoverian owes much to the German-born British kings of the House of Hanover. Between 1714 and 1820, they sent the finest English Thoroughbreds back to Germany to breed with descendants of the German Great Horse. The result was the Hanoverian, which is one of the finest showjumping horses in the world today.

AMERICAN QUARTER HORSE

This horse was bred by early settlers in America, in Virginia and Carolina. It has become famous for its success over quarter-mile races (about 400m) – hence its unusual name.

PONY PARADE

When fully grown, ponies are small horses. Nearly all those ridden today are descended from ponies which once roamed wild.

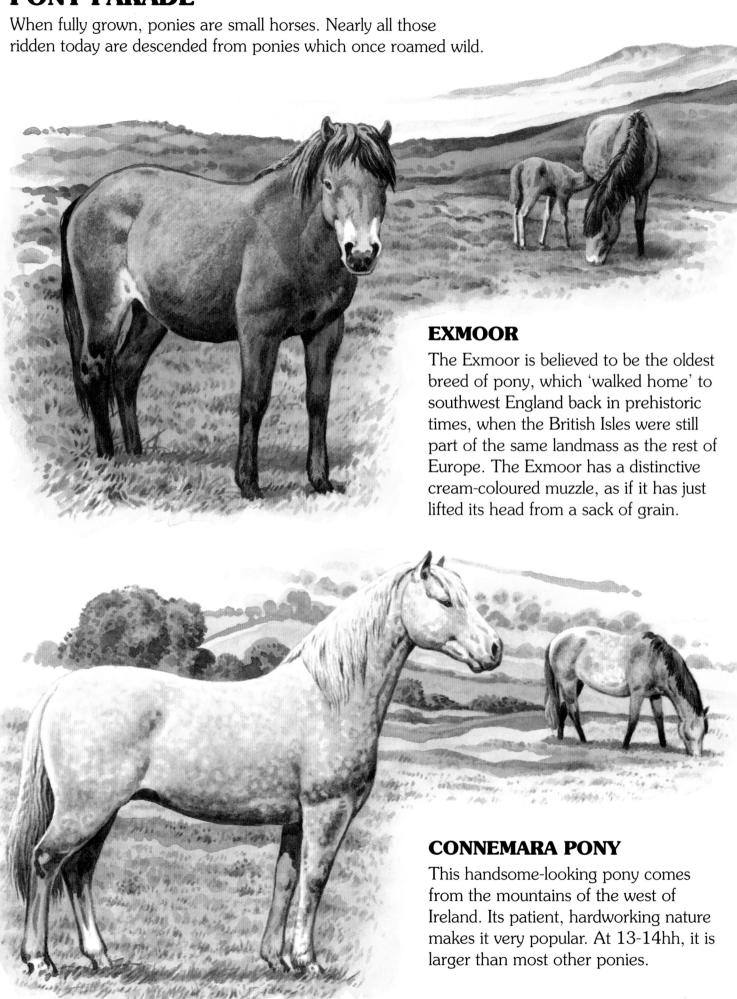

EXMOOR

The Exmoor is believed to be the oldest breed of pony, which 'walked home' to southwest England back in prehistoric times, when the British Isles were still part of the same landmass as the rest of Europe. The Exmoor has a distinctive cream-coloured muzzle, as if it has just lifted its head from a sack of grain.

CONNEMARA PONY

This handsome-looking pony comes from the mountains of the west of Ireland. Its patient, hardworking nature makes it very popular. At 13-14hh, it is larger than most other ponies.

WELSH MOUNTAIN PONY

It is said that Julius Caesar began breeding the Welsh Mountain Pony after he invaded Britain. Strong and hardworking, it was widely used as a pit pony, and is now a popular riding and show pony.

SHETLAND PONY

At around lOhh, the Shetland is one of the smallest breeds, but also one of the strongest. It has a thick, woolly coat, a thick mane, a forelock falling across the eyes, and, most noticeable of all, a long tail sweeping the ground.

DARTMOOR

This close neighbour of the Exmoor is popular with young riders because of its kind nature and its intelligence. The Dartmoor pony is easily recognised by its long, shaggy mane and tail.

WORLD-FAMOUS PONIES

There are many breeds of ponies which come from different parts of the world – and many reasons why they have become famous in countries far from their native home.

FALABELLA

At just 7hh, the Falabella is the smallest horse in the world. It is named after the Falabella family, who began the breed in Argentina just over 100 years ago, developing it from the Shetland Pony.

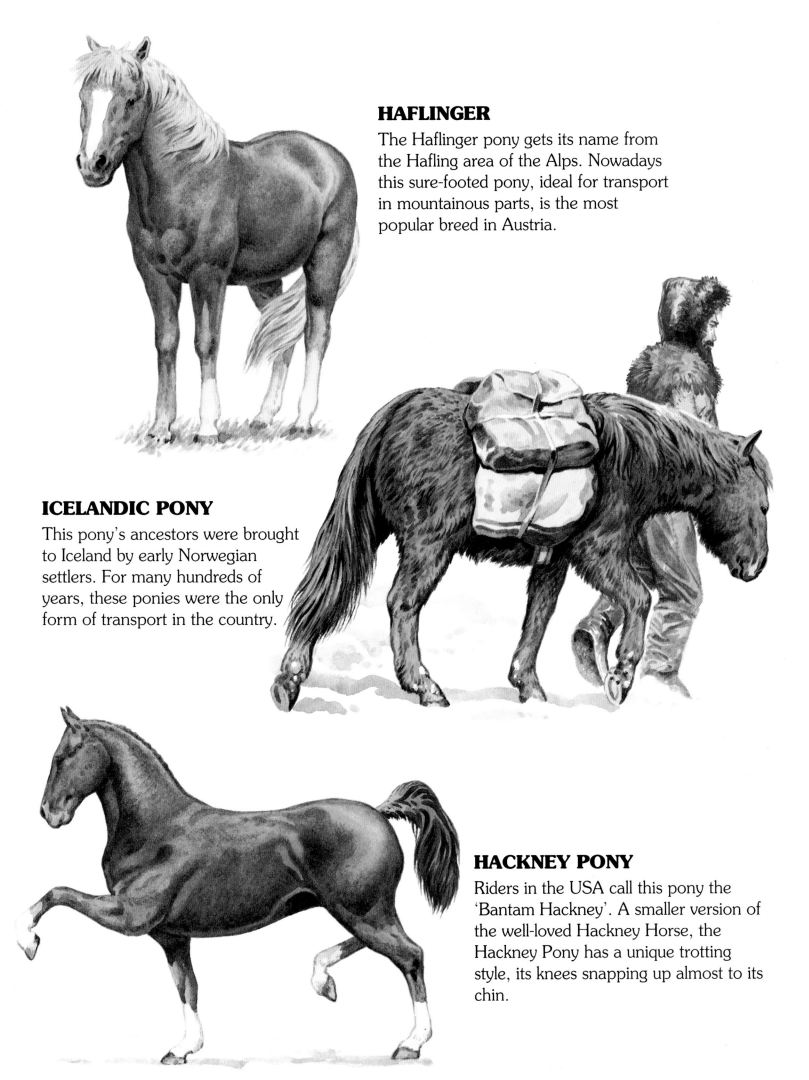

HAFLINGER

The Haflinger pony gets its name from the Hafling area of the Alps. Nowadays this sure-footed pony, ideal for transport in mountainous parts, is the most popular breed in Austria.

ICELANDIC PONY

This pony's ancestors were brought to Iceland by early Norwegian settlers. For many hundreds of years, these ponies were the only form of transport in the country.

HACKNEY PONY

Riders in the USA call this pony the 'Bantam Hackney'. A smaller version of the well-loved Hackney Horse, the Hackney Pony has a unique trotting style, its knees snapping up almost to its chin.

UNUSUAL HORSES

There are a number of very unusual horses throughout the world. Some are unusual because of their appearance, others because of their way of moving. Here are four of these 'unusual' breeds.

LUSITANO

This splendid-looking horse from Portugal is famous for its appearance in the bull-ring. In Portugal, bull-fighting is ceremonial and the bull is not harmed. The Lusitano is also used for farm-work throughout Spain and Portugal.

PINTO

The Spanish settlers in North America called this the 'Paint Horse' ('pinto' is Spanish for paint), which describes very well the horse's unusual piebald and skewbald colouring – as if its coat were splashed with paint.

KNABSTRUP

Denmark is the home of this unusual
spotted horse. The Knabstrup has a
long history as a circus horse.

PERUVIAN PASO

'Paso' is the Spanish for step, and it is
the way the Peruvian Paso moves which
makes it so unusual, flipping back its
front legs, its rear legs sweeping forward
in long strides. It is also called the
Peruvian Stepping Horse.

HEAVY HORSES

There are 23 breeds of heavy horses throughout the world. Some of them are termed 'draught horses', meaning horses which pull a vehicle. Most were bred especially for farming, and heavy horses are still used for ploughing in many countries.

PERCHERON

This horse was first bred in La Perche in Normandy, France, about 130 years ago. It is well-known, throughout most of Europe, Canada and the USA, for its great strength and docile nature.

SUFFOLK PUNCH

The famous Suffolk Punch dates back to the Middle Ages, making it one of the oldest breeds of heavy horse in the world. Used for both draught work and ploughing, its colour is always referred to as 'chesnut', a special spelling of the word, just for this fine horse.

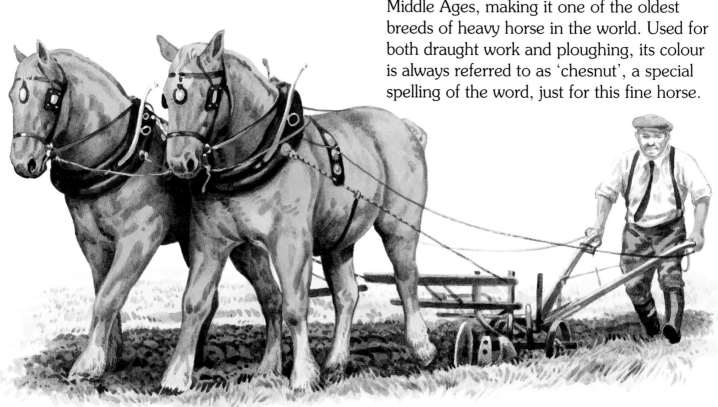

SHIRE HORSE

This is the most famous of heavy horses, popular all over the world. Placid and immensely strong, the Shire can pull weights of up to five tonnes. Whatever the body colour, all Shire Horses have white lower limbs and feet.

DUTCH HEAVY DRAUGHT

One of the largest of all heavy horses, with a massive, wide back and powerful limbs, the Dutch Heavy Draught is also one of the most recent breeds.

RACEHORSES

Horses have been raced for hundreds of years. Horse racing may have started for local amusement, but today it is both a sport and an industry, with classic horse races held all over the world.

HURDLES

Although hurdle racing began in Britain and Ireland, it is now popular in most parts of the world. Hurdles are 1.2 metres high, set out at four hurdles per kilometre.

FLAT RACING

In flat racing, horses race from 5 to 11 furlongs without jumps (a furlong is equivalent to 203 metres). Famous races include the English Derby, Australia's Melbourne Cup, and, in the USA, the Belmont Stakes.

TROTTING

Trotting races are seen in America, Australia, New Zealand, France, Italy, and in Russia, where they began. The horse is only permitted to trot, pulling a light, two-wheeled cart, called a 'sulky', in which the jockey is seated.

STEEPLECHASING

The steeplechase began as a cross-country race towards a church steeple, hence the name! Steeplechases are longer than flat races, with a set number of obstacles, including a water jump. Probably the world's most famous steeplechase is the Grand National, run each year at Aintree, near Liverpool, in England.

SHOWS AND COMPETITIONS

Horse shows and competitions are made up of different sections, like dressage and showjumping; and are of different kinds, like horse trials and gymkhanas.

SHOWJUMPING

Showjumping can take place inside a closed arena or out in the open. Apart from having a jumping ability, showjumpers have to be horses of speed.

HORSE TRIAL

As well as showjumping and dressage, horse trials include a cross-country event or steeplechase over fixed obstacles such as fences, hedges, and water hazards.

DRESSAGE

This is the most elegant of all competition events, in which rider and horse have to work together to achieve harmony in all movements, whether walking or trotting, coming to a halt, turning, or moving in a straight line.

GYMKHANA

A gymkhana is a competition for junior riders, and will usually include showjumping and novelty races.

THE HORSE AND FARMING

Before the arrival of the tractor, all farm haulage work was done by horses. In many parts of the world, farmers and growers still depend on the horse for their livelihood and survival.

HORSES AND CATTLE

Ever since men began herding cattle, horses have been used to round them up and to drive them. The most famous cattlemen are the cowboys of the USA and Mexico, and the Gauchos of Argentina in South America.

PACK-HORSES AND PONIES

These are the horses which carry heavy loads, particularly in mountainous regions where vehicles cannot go.

PLOUGHING

Many farmers still prefer to use heavy horses, such as the Shire and the Clydesdale, for ploughing, especially in rough or hilly areas where tractor driving is difficult.

HORSEWHEELS

In many parts of the world, teams of horses are still used to pull the wheels which provide power for mills to grind corn, or draw water from deep wells.

TRAVEL BY HORSE

For hundreds of years, ordinary people in many parts of the world depended on the horse for day-to-day travel.

TRAVEL BY BUS

Few motor cars were on the road when horse-drawn buses jostled for space with hackney carriages. These carriages were named after the Hackney Horses which pulled them, and were the forerunner of the taxi service.

TRAVEL BY COACH

Stagecoaches travelled from one town to another, picking up and setting down passengers. Only the richer people could afford this service, so highwaymen and outlaws soon saw an easy target in stagecoaches as they bumped over the rutted roads.

TRAVEL BY WAGON

For thousands of kilometres across North America, horses pulled the pioneer settlers in their covered wagons, which contained all their belongings, including the tools they needed to start a new life.

TRAVEL BY RAIL

To begin with, railway tracks were not laid for trains, but to enable horses to pull trucks and wagons along more easily. The first trams were also horse-drawn in this way.

HORSES AT WORK

Blacksmiths, or farriers, were once thought to have magic powers, because only they knew how to 'work' the iron for horseshoes. So they were always treated with respect, in case they had any magic to use against people they did not like! Few people could manage without the strength of a horse for long.

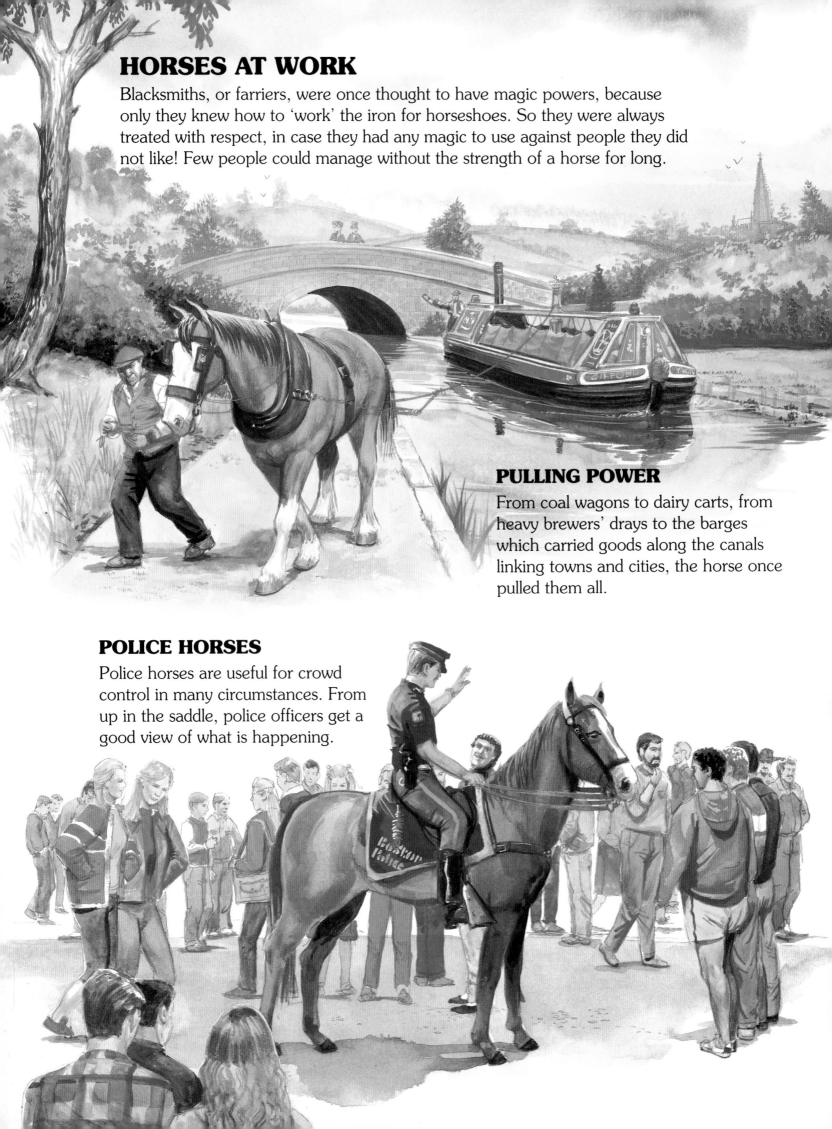

PULLING POWER

From coal wagons to dairy carts, from heavy brewers' drays to the barges which carried goods along the canals linking towns and cities, the horse once pulled them all.

POLICE HORSES

Police horses are useful for crowd control in many circumstances. From up in the saddle, police officers get a good view of what is happening.

PIT PONIES

Every coal mine once had pit ponies pulling heavily-loaded trucks underground. It is only in recent times that this labour has stopped, but ponies are still used in industry in some countries.

CARRIAGES AND COACHES

Many different types of carriages have been built worldwide, and some are used on state occasions even today. Carriage driving with teams of two or four horses is also an increasingly popular sport.

PERFORMING HORSES

There are few people who can resist the colour and spectacle of horses in a show. Sometimes, a horse is specially trained; at other times, the horse's performance is part of its nature; or it is really just doing a job of work.

LIPPIZANER HORSE

Lippizaners are the most famous horses in riding displays. The breed began with 9 stallions and 24 mares which were brought from Spain to Vienna in Austria, where the Spanish Riding School was founded in 1735.

HORSES ON PARADE

Military bands are often led by a rider seated on a horse, with a ceremonial drum on either side. Just imagine how calm and obedient a horse must be, whilst a great drum is beaten at full strength right behind its ears!

RODEO

The rodeo is a show in which American cowboys demonstrate their skill in riding the 'bucking bronco', or unbroken (untamed) horse. A 'bronco-buster' is a cowboy who tames and rides wild broncos, or mustangs.

TACK

When horse people talk about tack, they mean all the items needed to keep a horse clean and fit for work. Riders and horse owners often refer to tack as 'saddlery', and, after riding, every piece has to be carefully cleaned and put away in a special place, usually called the 'tack room'.

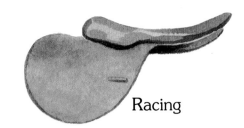

Racing

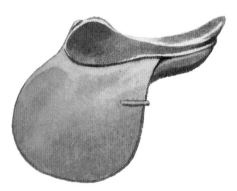

General

Jumping

Side-saddle

SADDLE

Different types of saddle include the lightweight racing saddle used by jockeys; side-saddles, which many female riders prefer; and the western saddle with the high 'pommel' in front, upon which a cowboy can keep a lasso. The most widely used is the general purpose saddle.

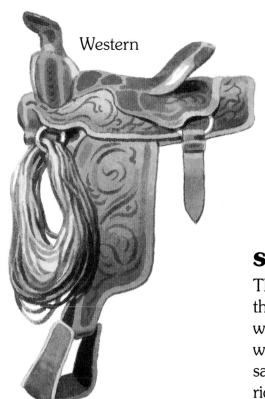

Western

STIRRUPS

There are three parts to each stirrup: the *Stirrup Leather*, an adjustable strap which goes through the *Stirrup Bar*, which is covered by the skirt flap on the saddle; and the *Stirrup Iron* for the rider's foot.

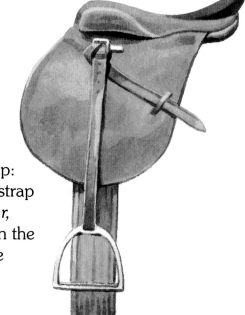

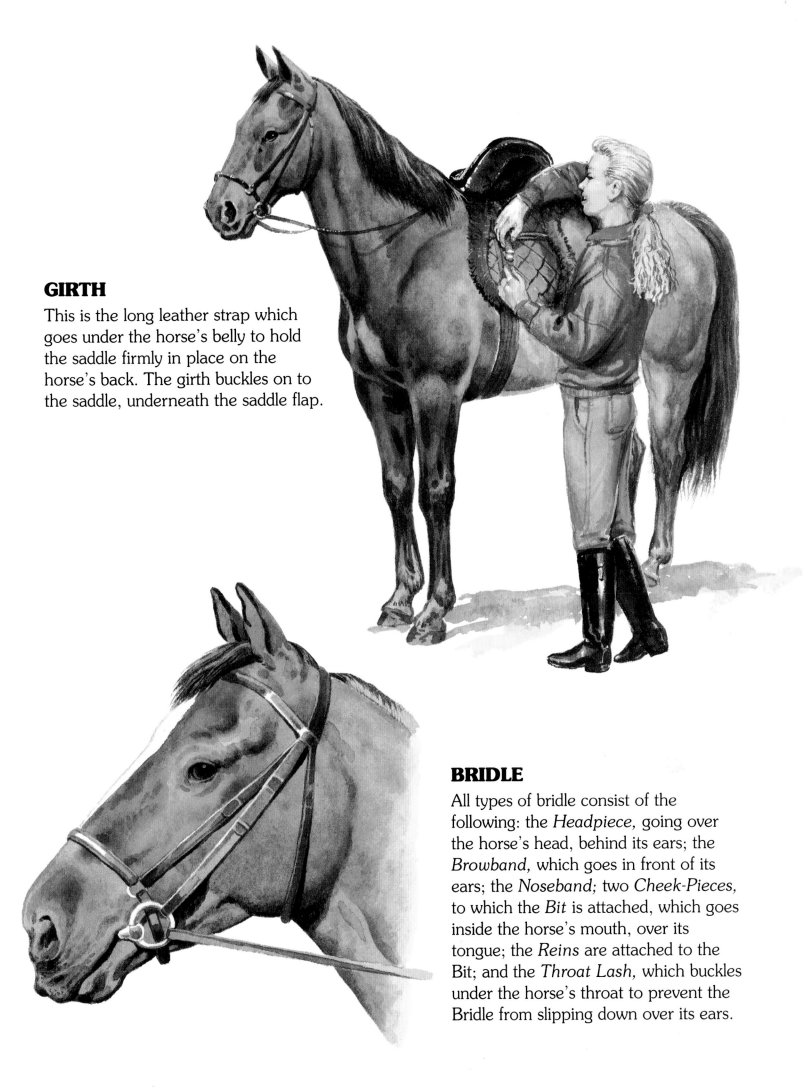

GIRTH

This is the long leather strap which goes under the horse's belly to hold the saddle firmly in place on the horse's back. The girth buckles on to the saddle, underneath the saddle flap.

BRIDLE

All types of bridle consist of the following: the *Headpiece*, going over the horse's head, behind its ears; the *Browband*, which goes in front of its ears; the *Noseband*; two *Cheek-Pieces*, to which the *Bit* is attached, which goes inside the horse's mouth, over its tongue; the *Reins* are attached to the Bit; and the *Throat Lash*, which buckles under the horse's throat to prevent the Bridle from slipping down over its ears.

CARE OF A HORSE

Almost everyone who is interested in horses has dreams of owning one. If you are ever lucky enough to see this dream coming true, do remember that, like any other animal, a horse takes a lot of looking after. Here are some important points to bear in mind.

GROOMING

It takes about half an hour to groom a horse before riding. Afterwards, a brisk rub-down will have to be followed by more grooming. Keeping a horse well-groomed and in good shape takes a great deal of time!

WHAT AGE?

Many ponies and horses are taken from their mothers far too early, making them nervous and difficult to handle. Riding a pony before it is three and a half to four years old could permanently damage its spine.

CHOOSING A HORSE OR PONY

Do go to a reputable stable – ask a local veterinary surgery for a recommendation. Then have a good look around to see what the animals are like. Do they seem contented and well looked after? Are the stables clean, with good exercise space for the horses? Do the horses seem interested in their surroundings?

SPACE

Any horse must have space for exercise as well as grazing. Even the tamest of horses will quickly become bad-tempered when it is cooped up for long periods.

POINTS OF A HORSE

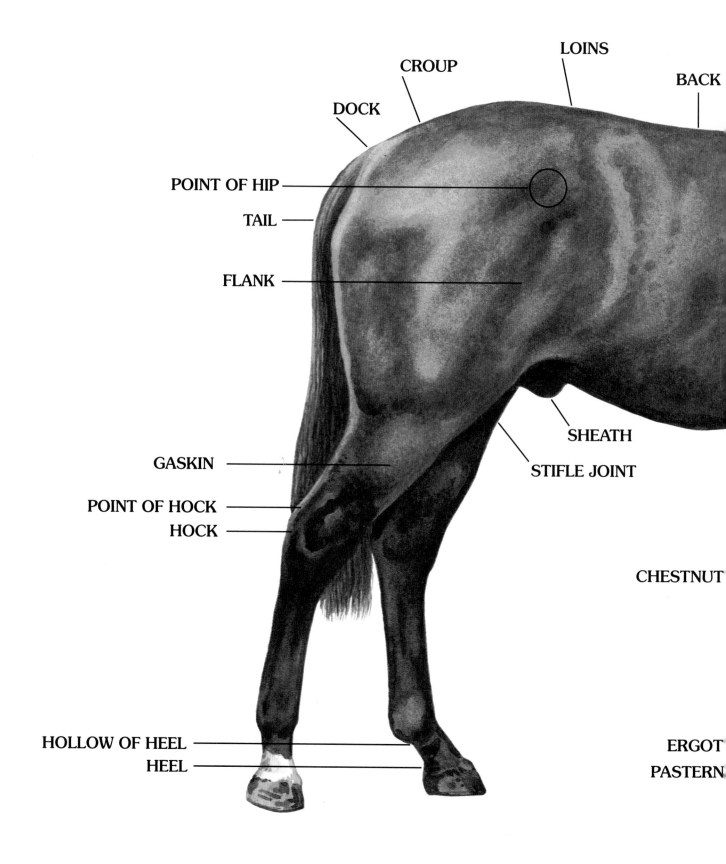

LOINS

CROUP

BACK

DOCK

POINT OF HIP

TAIL

FLANK

SHEATH

STIFLE JOINT

GASKIN

POINT OF HOCK

HOCK

CHESTNUT

HOLLOW OF HEEL

HEEL

ERGOT

PASTERN

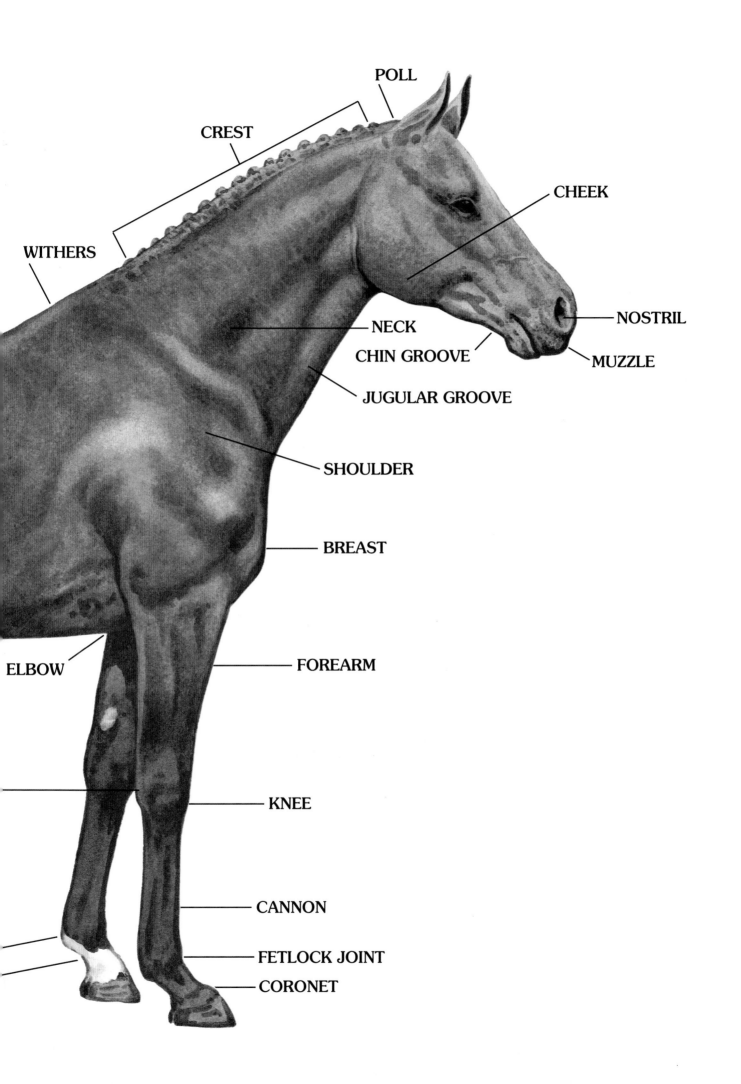

POLL

CREST

WITHERS

CHEEK

NOSTRIL

NECK

CHIN GROOVE

MUZZLE

JUGULAR GROOVE

SHOULDER

BREAST

ELBOW

FOREARM

KNEE

CANNON

FETLOCK JOINT

CORONET

ASSES, DONKEYS AND MULES

Although, perhaps, the most humble members of the horse family in terms of breeding, asses, donkeys and mules are the true 'beasts of burden', the working animals on whom the lives of people have depended for thousands of years.

ASS

Wild asses live in the deserts of northeast Africa. They are easily recognised by their long ears. The ass also has much smaller hooves than a horse.

ONAGER (or Asian Wild Ass)

Onagers can still be found in the wild, from the Middle East to the deserts of northwest India. Well over 2000 years ago, they were used for chariot racing, especially by the Assyrians.

MULE

Why is a Mule so strong? Because it gets its strength and toughness from its male donkey (jackass) father, and from its mare mother it inherits the size of a horse.

DONKEY

The Donkey is descended from the African Wild Ass. Being easier to keep and cheaper to feed than a horse, it is widely used in poor countries. Donkeys are also sure-footed, and so work well in rocky areas.

HORSES IN HISTORY

For many hundreds of years, until recent times, soldiers and explorers took horses with them wherever they went. The animals were often crowded together in ships and kept in terrible conditions below decks. Men always took more horses than they actually needed, knowing that many would not survive a long voyage. Untold numbers of horses have also perished alongside men in wars and battles throughout the course of history.

MONGOLS

In the 13th Century, led by Genghis Khan, the Mongols were among the finest horsemen ever known. After conquering a vast territory from China to Afghanistan, the Mongols moved into southeast Europe. Their empire extended from the Black Sea in the west to the Yellow Sea in the east.

THE CHARGE OF THE LIGHT BRIGADE

The Charge of the Light Brigade took place in 1854, during the Battle of Balaclava, in the Crimean War. Hundreds of cavalrymen and their horses were killed when the British Light Cavalry was ordered to charge the heavy cannons of the Russian Army.

KNIGHTS IN ARMOUR

The 12th Century Crusaders, in their 'holy war' on behalf of the Christian Church, were the first knights in armour. For centuries afterwards, throughout Europe, Asia, and North Africa, men wore armour in battle to protect both rider and horse.

CHARIOT RACING

Four-horse chariot races formed part of the Olympic Games in Greece in 7 BC. Centuries before that, the Ancient Romans had begun chariot racing around a special course called a 'hippodrome'.

HORSE FACT FILES

Pages 6-7: Types of Horse
COLOUR TYPES

Palomino: coat; cream: mane, tail; fair almost white
Dun-Yellow Dun: coat; golden-yellow to cream
   -Blue Dun: coat; blue-grey
Bay: coat; brown: mane, tail; black
Chestnut: coat; reddish brown: mane, tail; lighter
Roan-Strawberry Roan: coat; mixed chestnut and white hairs
   -Blue Roan: coat; brown, some white

Pages 8-9: Horses and Ponies on Show
THE HORSE FAMILY

Stallion: male, age 4+, able to sire a foal
Mare: female, age 4+
Sire: father of foal
Dam: mother of foal
Foal: baby horse, up to 12 months
Colt: male, up to 4 yrs old
Filly: female, up to 4 yrs old
Yearling: colt or filly, 12-23 months
Gelding: male foal which has been gelded, or castrated, so unable to sire a foal

Pages 10-11: Basic Types
HOW MANY 'HANDS' HIGH

A horse is measured in 'hands', from feet to shoulders, or 'withers'. One hand is the width of an adult hand, about 10.16cm. So, if a horse is 15.3hh (hh=hands high), its height is 1.61m. 15hh would be a small horse. Ponies average about 12.2hh.

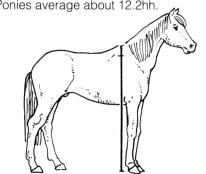

Pages 12-13: Classic Horses
ARAB HORSE HISTORY

All English thoroughbreds, now racing worldwide, are descended from three individual Arab horses.
Byerley Turk: brought to England 1689 by Capt. Robert Byerley
Darley Arabian: brought to England 1704 by Thomas Darley
Godolphin Arabian: brought to England 1732

Pages 14-15: Horses Around the World
HORSES IN STORY AND LEGEND

Horses appear in stories and legends from many places.
Celtic Goddess, Epòna, ruled over horses and ponies, often taking the form of a horse herself.
Norse God, Odin, rode across the sky on an eight-footed horse.
The Thracian Mares, in Greek legend, could run like the wind. They belonged to King Diomedes of Thrace, and were stolen by Hercules. All Greek and Turkish horses have ancient origins.
Pegasus, winged horse in Greek legend, was ridden by Bellerophon.

Pages 16-17: Pony Parade
PIEBALD AND SKEWBALD

These are particular types of colouring in horses and ponies.
Piebald: coat; spotted or patched, especially in black and white, in no particular pattern.
Skewbald: coat; irregular patches of white, or any colour except black.

Pages 18-19: World Famous Ponies
PONY PENNING DAY

Only wild ponies live on tiny Assateague Island, off the coast of Virginia, USA. Nobody knows how they got there. It is thought their ancestors were being taken from Africa to America, when their ship was wrecked, and the ponies swam ashore to the island. Each year, in July, men from nearby Chincoteague Island take their own horses over to Assateague, to capture some wild ponies, and bring them back, amidst great excitement. This is Pony Penning Day.

Black Bess, the legendary mount of English highwayman, Dick Turpin, was said to have been ridden by him over 300km non-stop from London to York.

Pages 20-21: Unusual Horses
UNUSUAL HORSE CUSTOMS

A horse's skull was often set into the topmost point of a Scandinavian house, to keep away ill-fortune.
An ancient cure for whooping cough was to let a piebald horse breathe on the sufferer. Many still believe a horse's breath is a cure for chest complaints.

Pages 22-23: Heavy Horses
LUCKY HORSESHOES

All horses need shoeing every 5-8 weeks, depending on their work and conditions underfoot.
For centuries, horseshoes have been symbols of good luck worldwide, because horses signified plenty, especially at harvest-time.
To 'keep good luck in', a horseshoe must be hung with its open part up.

Pages 24-25: Racehorses
RACING FACTS

Point-to-Point: Shares common origin with steeplechase; first race run across country from one 'point' to another. Now raced on a spectator course.
Most Famous Flat Race Ever: Probably the English Derby of June 1867. The winner *Hermit* had previously been near death, and a jockey was only found at the last minute.

Pages 26-27: Shows and Competitions
HORSES AND JUMPING

Horses and ponies are *not* natural jumpers, though most will usually clear a fence when they have to. For the show ring, they have to be specially trained, long before carrying a rider. All wear 'over-reach' bands on the front fetlocks to protect them from being struck during jumping by the hind shoes.

Pages 28-29: The Horse and Farming
HORSE POWER

An engine's strength is expressed as a measure of the pulling power of a horse. Horsepower is part of the specification of any vehicle.
Saddle Horses: These are horses that work on cattle stations, or ranches. The Australian Stock Horse, based on the Waler, is a famous breed of saddle horse.

Pages 30-31: Travel by Horse
STRAIGHT FROM THE HORSE'S MOUTH

Before telegraph cables and phone lines, news was carried by riders on horseback, or by coach. Along stagecoach routes, coaching inns were also postal stations, where letters and goods could be left, to be taken onwards by coach.
Pony Express: Briefly, in America in the mid-1800s, this was a fast postal service between Missouri and California.

Pages 32-33: Horses at Work
WORKING FACTS

Tow Paths: Paths beside rivers and canals, along which horses would trudge, towing barges.
Cock Horse: If a load was too heavy for a team of horses, especially going uphill, an extra horse, called a 'cock horse' or 'trace horse', was harnessed to the front.

Pages 34-35: Performing Horses
ON THEIR BEST BEHAVIOUR

Rodeo: Began as riding or roping contests between cowboys taking part in horse or cattle round-ups. Before branding, animals were held in enclosure called a 'rodeo', so contests became known as rodeos. During a round-up, cowboys relied fully on the skill and obedience of their well-trained cow ponies.
Drumming up Support: Phrase comes from army tradition of drummer on horseback urging soldiers on during a battle.

Pages 36-37: Tack
GROOMING

Grooming Kit: Kept in 'Tack Room'.
Brushes -Dandy: Removes heavy dirt.
       -Body: Brushes dirt and dust from coat, mane, and tail.
       -Wet: For mane, tail, feet.
Curry Comb: Mainly for cleaning the Body Brush.
Hoof Pick: Removes dirt or stones from hoofs.

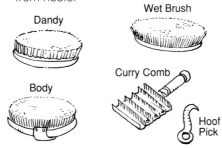

Dandy   Wet Brush   Curry Comb   Body   Hoof Pick

Pages 38-39: Care of a Horse
MONEY IS NEEDED FOR . . .

Winter Feed: Hay and fodder.
Winter Stabling: If needed.
Vets' Fees: Healthiest horse needs the vet at least once a year!
Blacksmith's Fees: Horses need shoeing at least every 6 weeks.
Insurance: For horse, and in case it damages someone's property.
Tack: Saddle, bridle, reins, etc.
Riding Hat and Boots
PLUS entry fees for competitions, etc; loose boxes; jodhpurs and jacket, if you are competing!

Pages 40-41: Points of a Horse
PHYSICAL FACTS

Feathering: Shaggy tuft of hair growing behind fetlock, and usually hanging down over hoof. Shire Horses and Shetland Ponies are breeds with feathering.
Blaze: Broad, white marking between eyes, running all down face.
Teeth: As it ages, horse's teeth change in shape and size, which is how you can tell its age. Most easily seen is way that gums shrink back as horse gets older, making teeth seem longer. That is why, when someone gets older, we say they are 'long in the tooth'!

Pages 42-43: Asses, Donkeys and Mules
MULES AND HINNIES

Mules: Sterile, cannot produce young, not amongst themselves, nor with horses.
Hinnies: Offspring of 'jenny', a female donkey, and male horse. Hinnies are rarer than mules.
Both have reputation for being stubborn, but are brave and hard-working.

Pages 44-45: Horses in History
WARS AND WEALTH

Bucephalus: Alexander the Great's black stallion. Carried Alexander during conquest of Asia Minor, Persia (now Iran), and to India, an immense journey even by modern transport. Horse died in 326BC after battle on Hydaspes River. Alexander founded city of Bucephala in horse's honour.
Marengo: Grey Arab pony, Napoleon's favourite. He rode it throughout Battle of Waterloo in 1815.
Cavalry Horses: Ridden in battle until very recent times. Word 'cavalry' of French origin; they are the 'horse soldiers'.
Waler: Finest cavalry horse of World War I; from New South Wales in Australia.
Ponies and Mules: In World War II, used in Africa, Italy, and Burma to carry ammunition and supplies through mountainous regions.
Richest Horse in History: Probably *Incitatus,* favourite of Roman emperor Caligula (AD12-41). He showered riches on horse, including marble stail; solid gold pail, for water; manger carved from ivory. Caligula also made *Incitatus* a Roman Citizen and a Senator!

Index